W9-CVA-096

FARMLAND INNOVATOR

A Creative Minds Biography

FARMLAND INNOVATOR

A Story about Cyrus McCormick

by Catherine A. Welch

illustrations by Jan Naimo Jones

M Millbrook Press/Minneapolis

To John and Gloria—C.A.W.

Special thanks to Lee Grady and Alexis Ernst-Treutel of the Wisconsin
Historical Society for providing primary source material from the
McCormick-International Harvester Collection. The author also wishes to
thank Judith Stark, Raymond Bouley, Jacqueline Hoffman, Katherine
Mostacero, and the staff of the Southbury, Connecticut, library for their
assistance in gathering material for this book.

Millbrook Press, Inc.
A division of Lerner Publishing Group
241 First Avenue North
Minneapolis, MN 55401 U.S.A.

Website address: www.lernerbooks.com

Library of Congress Cataloging-in-Publication Data

Welch, Catherine A.
     Farmland Innovator : a story about Cyrus McCormick / by
Catherine A. Welch ; illustrations by Jan Naimo Jones.
        p.   cm. — (A creative minds biography)
     Includes bibliographical references and index.
     ISBN-13: 978–0–8225–5988–7 (lib. bdg. : alk. paper)
     ISBN-10: 0–8225–5988–9 (lib. bdg. : alk. paper)
     1. McCormick, Cyrus Hall, 1809–1884—Juvenile literature.
     2. Inventors—United States—Biography—Juvenile literature.
     3. Harvesting machinery—United States—History—Juvenile literature.
     I. Jones, Jan Naimo, ill. II. Title. III. Series.
     HD9486.U6M339 2007
     681'.7631092—dc22   2006000416

Manufactured in the United States of America
1 2 3 4 5 6 – JR – 12 11 10 09 08 07

Table of Contents

1

Dreams at Walnut Grove

Fifteen-year-old Cyrus Hall McCormick dreaded the wheat harvest. Hour after hour, he stooped in the scorching hot fields with the workers. Sweat streamed down his face as he swung the heavy cradle. SWISH, SWISH, SWISH. Over and over, he cut and tossed the wheat stalks. The long-bladed cradle was the best tool that farmers had for harvesting grain. But Cyrus's body ached after each day's work.

Cyrus didn't like laboring in the fields. He was a thinker. He liked to solve problems. So Cyrus thought about a way to make his job easier. He crafted a smaller and lighter cradle for himself. It was easier to swing, and his muscles weren't as sore. But the work in the fields still seemed endless.

Cyrus's father, Robert McCormick, was a thinker too. Some people said he was a genius. More than anything, he liked to tinker with machines. He always had a few inventions in the works. Around the time Cyrus was born in 1809, Mr. McCormick started a new invention—a wheat-cutting machine. As a young boy, Cyrus watched his father work on this machine.

Cyrus saw his father's invention fail time after time. Mr. McCormick often pushed aside the wheat-cutting machine to work on other inventions. But Cyrus saw that he never gave up. His father always came back to the machine and tinkered some more.

The McCormick farm—called Walnut Grove—lay in Rockbridge County, Virginia. The farm provided nearly everything the Scotch-Irish family needed. Wool, cotton, and the fibers of flax plants were spun into yarn to make cloth. When the family wanted lumber for building, they cut logs at their sawmill. Water-powered machines ground their grain into flour at their gristmill. The smokehouse preserved meat from cattle and hogs. And there was a blacksmith shop for making iron into tools and horseshoes. Cyrus grew up learning that hard work had its rewards.

Walnut Grove had been the family home for many years. Cyrus's great-grandfather once farmed the land. At first, Cyrus's family lived in a log house. But when the McCormick family grew, they moved into a large redbrick house. The new place had plenty of room for Cyrus and his brothers and sisters—William, Mary Caroline, Leander, John, and Amanda.

The McCormicks and their neighbors lived in a quiet valley. Their farms stood far away from cities and towns. People traveled by horse on rough clay roads. Neighbors helped each other. They gathered to husk corn. They threw house-raising parties where everyone worked together to quickly build a farmhouse. And they harvested crops together. Everyone went to church on Sundays. For a while, Cyrus was the lead singer in his Presbyterian church. Services lasted all day.

Cyrus didn't always fit in with his neighbors. The valley folks dressed plainly. Some went to church barefoot. Cyrus was a snappy dresser. He wore a broadcloth coat and a black beaver hat to church. Some people said Cyrus thought he was better than everyone else. He *was* better in some ways. Young men in the valley often drank and smoked. But Cyrus never did. After a hard day's work, he played tunes on his fiddle.

Sometimes Cyrus would help his father mold iron in the blacksmith shop. But Cyrus liked using his head, not his hands. He would help a little and get his hands soiled a bit. But he didn't throw himself into the work like his father did. Mr. McCormick was always covered in soot and grime when he left the shop.

Cyrus wanted to learn new things. He spent his spare time reading. He had a special tutor to teach him mathematics and how to survey property. He learned to measure the boundaries, area, and height of the land. But Cyrus learned the most by helping his father. Running the homestead was like running a business. Cyrus saw how Walnut Grove was a success. By the late 1820s, Mr. McCormick owned 1,200 acres of land and eighteen horses. Like many landowners at that time, he also owned slaves. Nine slaves worked the McCormick farm.

Cyrus was a lot like his father. But he had much of his mother in him too. Her name was Mary Ann, but everyone called her Polly. Both Cyrus and his mother were full of energy. Mrs. McCormick loved to drive her carriage briskly across the rough roads. Cyrus pushed his spirited horse to high speeds too. Like her son, Mrs. McCormick dressed well and took pride in her family's stylish belongings.

Mrs. McCormick was strong-willed, and Cyrus was the same. He couldn't be talked out of an idea once he got it into his head. Mrs. McCormick had high hopes for Cyrus. She said that Cyrus was smart and had a good head for business. He wouldn't be happy puttering in a shop. She believed Cyrus had a gift for talking and could make people listen to his ideas.

Mrs. McCormick was sure Cyrus would leave Virginia someday and do more important things. Cyrus knew it too. He didn't want to spend his whole life at Walnut Grove. He had big dreams. He dreamed of traveling beyond the Blue Ridge Mountains. He dreamed of living in a grand house in a big city. He dreamed of servants and fancy clothes. He dreamed of being rich.

So Cyrus jumped at any chance to leave the farm. Sometimes he brought livestock to trade in the nearby towns of Lexington and Staunton. The trip was only eighteen miles. But that was far enough to catch a glimpse of the outside world. Cyrus met travelers passing through in stagecoaches. He could hear local politicians boom out speeches from the courthouse steps. And he could watch pioneers head west in covered wagons.

Cyrus always came back to Walnut Grove with his head full of new ideas. He was determined to make his fortune. He started thinking about his father's inventions. Mr. McCormick was still working on the wheat-cutting machine. Maybe, Cyrus thought, this wheat-cutting invention—this reaper machine—could make his family rich!

2

The Reaper Gift

Cyrus and his father knew farmers needed a reaper. Harvesting wheat, oats, and rye with hand tools was slow work. Farmers had only ten days to harvest ripe grain before it went bad. First, a worker had to cut the grain stalks with a cradle, which had a long cutting blade. Four long wooden "fingers" ran alongside the blade to catch the wheat as it was cut. The worker then swung the cradle and threw the cut grain into rows. Other workers followed to rake and tie the stalks into bundles.

It took about fifteen workers to cut, gather, and bind ten acres of wheat a day. This job took longer if the wheat was tangled or wet. Imagine how much time a cutting machine would save! With a horse-drawn reaper, farmers could harvest more grain with fewer workers. But Mr. McCormick had been tinkering with his invention for twenty years. He still didn't have a reaper that worked.

In 1828 Cyrus's cousin, William S. McCormick, came to work in the shops at Walnut Grove. William and a man named Samuel Hite helped Mr. McCormick with the reaper. Mr. McCormick did the thinking while William and Samuel did the building. The men toiled over the invention for months. Finally, they found success! The reaper could cut wheat. But Mr. McCormick wasn't satisfied. The reaper didn't properly cut tangled or overripe grain. It didn't work well on uneven ground. And it tended to stall. So everyone in the shop kept working.

In the meantime, Cyrus thought about selling his father's inventions. Mr. McCormick had dreamed up many practical tools. He built a special kind of black-smith bellows. This tool pumped out bursts of air to keep the shop fires hot. He also improved the thresher. This machine separated grains from stalks. Mr. McCormick's hemp-brake made it easier to break up harvests of hemp, a plant mostly used to make rope. He also invented a hydraulic engine—an engine powered by water. And then there was the reaper. A fine-working reaper could bring in big profits.

Mrs. McCormick had plans for the reaper too. She knew her husband was a talented inventor. But he didn't have Cyrus's passion for business and making money. And Mrs. McCormick thought that her son would leave Walnut Grove soon. She wanted to give Cyrus a good reason to stay. So Mrs. McCormick asked her husband to give his reaper invention to Cyrus.

At first, Mr. McCormick didn't like this plan. After all, the reaper was his creation. He had worked on it for twenty years. And the reaper might make a lot of money. Why should Cyrus get rich off the invention? Mr. McCormick wanted all his children to share in the success. Cyrus agreed. He would build a business that would benefit the entire McCormick family.

Cyrus turned twenty-one in 1830. That year Mr. McCormick gave him the reaper. Cyrus and his father became partners in a machine business called Robert McCormick & Son. They were happy being partners. Mr. McCormick stayed at Walnut Grove with his inventions. Cyrus handled sales. He spread the word to farmers about the McCormick machines.

Cyrus and his father knew some inventors already had patents on machines. With a patent, only the inventor could make and sell an invention. Mr. McCormick wasn't ready to patent the reaper. But he thought McCormick & Son could make money from two other inventions—the hemp-brake and the hydraulic engine. Mr. McCormick would have to bring models of his machines to Washington, D.C., and pay a patent fee of $30 for each invention.

In July 1830, Cyrus went to Washington, D.C., with his father and his cousin William. The men made their way to the United States Patent Office. A room there held about two thousand small-scale models of American mechanical inventions. Some of the models were grain-cutting machines. But no inventor—here or in Europe—had a cutting machine that worked well. Cyrus left Washington eager to improve the McCormick reaper.

On October 1, 1830, the government granted Mr. McCormick's patents for the hydraulic engine and the hemp-brake. During the fall and winter, Robert McCormick & Son busied itself producing bellows and plows to sell. Cyrus and his father also worked on the hemp-brake machine. Cyrus thought this invention would be a big seller now that more farmers in the region were planting hemp.

By the spring of 1831, Mr. McCormick had a new reaper ready to test. It had a wooden framework and two wheels. Another part reeled in grain to be cut by a blade. Cut grain fell on a platform. A worker could walk alongside the platform to rake off the cut grain. Other workers then bundled the wheat. This improved reaper cut wheat cleaner, neater, and faster than a worker harvesting with a cradle. But Mr. McCormick still didn't think it was ready to sell.

Cyrus claimed that his father abandoned the reaper at this point. So Cyrus decided to build a reaper himself, with the help of a slave named Joe Anderson. Cyrus laid out his plans on big sheets of paper. Then he made small models of the machine. Cyrus used loose grain to test the models.

Cyrus claimed that he designed and built his new reaper in only six weeks. He said he added a gathering reel and a better divider bar at the end of the blade. In July 1831, Cyrus tested a full-size machine. Horses pulled the machine, which created a stir with its rattling noise. The reaper entertained the small crowd gathered. But no one saw it as the wonder machine farmers eagerly awaited. The machine sank in soft ground and stopped when it clogged with grain.

The reapers Cyrus and his father tested in 1831 cut grain, but neither worked well. Farmers needed something better. So the McCormicks put aside the reaper and set a different plan to make money. They thought the hemp-brake machine would bring in a lot of cash. Hemp was a big crop in Kentucky, so that's where Cyrus would go.

Farmers in Kentucky sold the hemp fibers to be made into coarse clothing, bagging, and twine. But hemp was hard to harvest. Preparing the plant fibers for the loom was tricky too. Farmers had to beat particles of stalk from the fibers. A hemp-brake machine would help clean these fibers.

By October 1, 1831, Cyrus was riding horseback through Kentucky. He carried drawings of the hemp-brake machine. Cyrus didn't plan to build a lot of these machines. Instead, he wanted to sell farmers the rights to build the invention on their own. But Cyrus knew farmers would want to see how the machine worked before buying it. But there was no way to move the invention from Walnut Grove to Kentucky. So Cyrus would have to build a hemp-brake machine.

Cyrus faced problems in Kentucky. Building the machines took longer and cost more there. And Cyrus couldn't build a machine that worked. He wished his father were there. Mr. McCormick wrote his son a detailed letter about an improved part for the machine. He explained how to make it, assemble it, and install it. Mr. McCormick warned Cyrus to keep all parts of the machine well oiled.

Cyrus tried and tried to build the machine, but he failed. He just didn't have the mechanical talent of his father. Still, Cyrus wanted to stay in Kentucky. He wanted to try building and selling the hydraulic engine his father had patented. But the McCormicks couldn't afford another business project. In May 1832, a disappointed Cyrus returned home.

3

Reapers in the News

Back in Walnut Grove, Cyrus decided it was time to advertise. In January 1833, he placed a newspaper ad in the *Lexington Union* newspaper to tell farmers about his hillside plow. Cyrus had improved an existing plow and patented his invention. While Mr. McCormick made plows, Cyrus started selling them. Cyrus also worked to make a name for himself. He wanted people to think of him as an inventor.

That summer Cyrus tested the reaper again. The machine didn't work perfectly. But Cyrus wanted to prove that the reaper *did* work. Soon he might have a reaper to sell. He wanted the public to know about his efforts. A story about Cyrus's reaper appeared in the September 14, 1833, issue of the *Union*. The headline called the reaper an "Important Invention" and named Cyrus as the inventor. Some people say the story wasn't a real news article with facts checked by a reporter. Maybe Cyrus gave the information to the newspaper himself.

Statements by three farmers appeared with the article. They said the machine operated well on ground that was free of stumps and rocks. They said the reaper cut about one acre an hour. Later, Cyrus used these statements in newspaper ads. Then other newspapers picked up the story. News about the McCormick reaper appeared in the *Mechanics' Magazine* of New York and the *Farmer's Register* of Richmond, Virginia. It was just the attention that Cyrus wanted.

But Cyrus wasn't the only man showing off a reaper invention. On December 31, 1833, Obed Hussey of Ohio patented a grain cutter. Hussey's machine worked much like the McCormick reaper, but his model wasn't perfect either. Hussey's reaper worked best if the two horses pulling the machine trotted. The trotting horses tired easily. And the Hussey reaper didn't have a reel like the McCormick model did. Harvesting grain that blew in the wind or bent away from the machine was hard. The McCormick reel pulled the stalks into the machine to be cut.

An article about Hussey's reaper appeared in the April 1834 issue of *Mechanics' Magazine*. The news hit Cyrus hard. What if people rushed out and bought the Hussey reaper? Cyrus had to act fast. On May 20 he sent a letter to *Mechanics' Magazine*. It stated that he, Cyrus McCormick, was the inventor of the first successful reaper. He wrote that he had tested his reaper on wheat and oats in July 1831 in front of witnesses. He warned that Hussey had no right to sell a reaper that was like the McCormick machine.

Cyrus's plans changed. He had wanted to build a better reaper before applying for a patent. Instead, he needed to rush his invention to the patent office. Cyrus wrote a report pointing out how his 1831 reaper differed from Hussey's. Most importantly, the McCormick reaper had a reel. But Cyrus didn't think that was good enough. So he included some optional changes that could be made to the reaper. He drew plans showing how horses could push the reaper rather than pull it. He also added a second blade. Called a knife, this blade would vibrate in the opposite direction of the first blade.

Cyrus raced to Washington, D.C. The government issued a patent for his reaper on June 21. The changes Cyrus added helped him get the patent, but these changes didn't make the reaper work better. In fact, they weren't even included in future McCormick reapers. But having the patent helped Cyrus claim the reaper as his own invention. He could show that his reaper was different from the one his father had given him.

Summer brought another harvest. Cyrus showed the reaper to farmers in several Virginia communities. Again, he asked farmers to write statements praising the reaper. Their thoughts appeared in more McCormick & Son newspaper ads. But farmers weren't convinced. They still weren't rushing to buy the machine—or any other machine, for that matter. McCormick & Son wasn't making enough money to stay in business.

Cyrus turned twenty-six in 1835. His future looked unsure. The machine business was failing, and he had no other career plans. He liked being in charge and being independent. And he was determined to find success. Maybe, he thought, it was time to leave. His brother William was twenty and managed all the farmwork. Leander was sixteen and talented with tools. Surely William and Leander could take care of all the daily jobs at Walnut Grove.

Mrs. McCormick liked having Cyrus around. She thought perhaps Cyrus would stay in Virginia if he had his own farm. So Robert and Polly McCormick gave Cyrus the 473 acres of Walnut Grove known as South River Farm. Along with the land, Mr. McCormick gave his son animals, tools, and seed.

Cyrus had always hated farming. But maybe running a farm all his own would be different. Crops, livestock, and other farm products sold well in 1835. Cyrus made good money from his first harvest. But he still thought farming was slow work. Cyrus was bored. He needed more excitement.

Mr. McCormick and Leander kept adding improvements to the reaper. But Cyrus didn't think much about the machine anymore. He had other ideas. Cyrus had a few thousand dollars saved, which he planned to invest in the iron business. Iron ore deposits existed all over the mountains of Virginia. Cyrus saw how money piled up for ironmasters. He wanted to be like these admired and respected men.

In 1836 Cyrus and his father created a new iron business called R. & C. H. McCormick. Daniel Matthews—a man who had experience in the iron industry—agreed to work for the McCormicks. Cyrus was in charge. The new business was exciting, and he worked hard. He even helped the workmen cut brush and haul stones. They cleared a space to build a smelter, which was called Cotopaxi Furnace. The smelter was a type of factory with tools for separating iron from the rock called ore.

Cotopaxi Furnace opened for business in the summer of 1837. But it wasn't long before R. & C. H. McCormick had troubles. Cyrus didn't know anything about the iron industry. He was young and inexperienced at running a business. He didn't get along with the workers he hired. And he didn't even know how to keep track of money coming into and out of the business. He made a mess of the company's financial records. Matthews knew all about the iron business, but Cyrus didn't listen to his advice.

Mr. McCormick and Leander had some duties at Cotopaxi Furnace. But they mostly labored in the workshops at Walnut Grove. The reaper was never far from their minds. Leander made several improvements. He rebuilt the reaper's frame near the cutter bar. He added parts to stop the knife when it wasn't in use. And he attached another part that held the knife in place. Each harvest, Leander and his father tested the reaper on their own grain crops.

During these years, the United States began spreading westward. By 1839 there were twenty-six states. Many Americans journeyed west to the open prairies. Cyrus heard that grain grew better there. Reaping machines would work well on the flatter land. Farmers started coming around to the idea of the reaper. They wanted better ways to grow crops and machines that would do the work faster.

By this time, the iron business was a failure. But Cyrus still didn't give up on his dreams. He was still determined to be rich one day. Once again, he turned his attention to the reaper. He tested the improved machine in public demonstrations. Leander's adjustments helped the reaper cut grain better than any McCormick machine so far.

Farming magazines and local newspapers began featuring more stories about reapers. These machines became big talk among farmers. Hussey was Cyrus's main competition. Hussey advertised and received the most attention. Farmers thought his reaper was perfect for dry wheat. But they complained that the cutter clogged if grain was damp. And Hussey's machine wouldn't reap at all if stalks bent away from the knife.

The McCormick reaper still had its own share of problems. The vibrating knife cut in only one direction. The reel wasn't braced securely. Sometimes the cut stalks wouldn't land on the platform properly, making the machine choke and stop. The reaper had to move as fast as the horses could pull it to prevent these problems. But then the reel spun too fast and scattered grain all over the field.

Cyrus had no idea how to fix the reaper. He left the mechanical work to his father and Leander. By 1841 they had solved all the problems, except one. They still had to deal with the vibrating knife that cut in only one direction.

4

War of the Reapers

Mr. McCormick and Leander worked on the vibrating knife problem. Cyrus taught farmers, field hands, and slaves how to use the reaper. The workers needed to train horses and mules. These animals weren't used to pulling a rattling machine. CLACK, CLACK, CLACK. This rumbling noise terrified the horses. Unless the animals were well trained, they would try to race ahead to escape the noise.

Before long, Cyrus gave farmers printed directions for the use and care of the reaper. Farmers must sharpen the knife after every fifty acres of grain they cut. The moving parts of the reaper had to be oiled frequently. Workers had to avoid driving the reaper against stumps and stones. And farmers must protect the machines from the weather. Cyrus would not guarantee how well the reaper would work. But he was willing to repair any machine that broke down because of poor construction. And he offered to replace any poorly made blade with a better one.

While Cyrus worked with the farmers, a blacksmith named John McCown pondered the vibrating knife problem. McCown's shop produced the McCormicks' reaper blades. McCown knew the McCormicks wanted a blade that could cut in both directions. One night McCown jumped out of bed with an idea. He hurried to his shop to work on the knife. McCown tried slanting the serrations in the blade. These notches looked like teeth on the edge of the blade. McCown cut some of the notches to the right and others to the left. He changed the direction of the slant every few inches. The knife would cut in both directions as it vibrated. This improvement doubled the amount of cutting power. The machine didn't choke as often either.

Leander always gave John McCown credit as the inventor of the two-way serrated knife. But Cyrus kept quiet about McCown's work. In fact, Cyrus took out a patent on this invention and paid McCown only for the work he had done. He even gave the contract for making the blades to another shop. Friends and family members urged McCown to fight for the rights to the patent, but he never did.

With the new blade in place, the McCormick reaper worked very well. In 1842 Cyrus started offering farmers a guarantee when they purchased the machine. In advertisements, he promised that the reaper would cut fifteen acres a day. If it didn't, Cyrus would repair the machine, replace it, or let farmers return it. The guarantee made sales rise.

To increase sales even more, Cyrus entered the McCormick machine in reaper races around the state. These festive events entertained crowds with contests and music. Cyrus entered a highly polished McCormick reaper. He used the best-trained workers and horses. The contests often weren't fair, though. The judges usually owned reapers and had their own favorite machines. But the McCormick reaper won sometimes. After each contest, Cyrus put the news of his victories in advertisements and on posters.

Both Cyrus and Hussey battled to get farmers' attention and money. Cyrus sold his reaper for about $105. Hussey offered a small machine for $100 and a larger machine for $170. In 1843 Hussey wrote a letter to the editor of the Richmond *Southern Planter*. The letter challenged Cyrus to a contest in the field. Farmers in the Richmond area buzzed about the challenge. The Reverend Jesse W. Turner arranged for a contest to be held on June 30. On June 24, 1843, Cyrus wrote a letter to the editor of the Richmond *Enquirer*. He formally challenged Hussey to the June 30 contest. The farmers would decide which reaper was best.

Hussey was eager for the challenge. A few days before the contest, Cyrus was working his reaper in a farmer's fields. Hussey showed up and announced that he wanted to challenge Cyrus right then and there. As a small crowd gathered, Cyrus began cutting the wheat. Then a sudden rain shower drenched the grain. Hussey's machine failed after the rain. It couldn't cut the wet grain.

On June 30, Cyrus and Hussey met for the contest as planned. Cyrus was lucky again. Hussey had to bring his smaller machine. High water had swept away a bridge before Hussey could get the larger machine across the James River and to the field.

The McCormick reaper cut seventeen acres that day. Hussey's small machine cut two acres and didn't work well in tangled grain. Hussey's larger machine would have done better. Still, farmers favored the McCormick reaper. It used only two horses, while Hussey's large machine needed three or four. The McCormick machine cost less than Hussey's larger machine. And the McCormick reaper cut damp grain better than Hussey's. Cyrus won the contest.

Business boomed at Walnut Grove in 1843. That year farmers in Virginia bought twenty-nine McCormick reapers. Mr. McCormick and his sons Leander and William worked hard in the factory at

Walnut Grove. Mr. McCormick owned the factory, and Cyrus took care of all the sales. Cyrus was thirty-four years old and was finally starting to make his dreams come true. He had high hopes for the reaper.

Cyrus started thinking about ways to sell the reaper in other states. He knew his father and brothers couldn't build all the reapers they would need. Even if they could, there was no good way to transport the machines. No railroad served the area around Walnut Grove. So Cyrus decided to sell the rights to build the reaper to others.

On October 27, 1843, he placed a notice in the *Richmond Semi-Weekly Whig*. He announced that he would sell patent rights for the machine. He was looking for partners to manufacture the reaper. Cyrus got a quick response. He sold rights for sixteen Virginia counties, one Maryland county, and one Michigan county. Cyrus would receive a twenty-dollar license fee for each reaper built. By January 1, 1844, Cyrus had raked in at least two thousand dollars in cash. This money helped finance the Walnut Grove factory and pay off debts from the iron business.

In June, Cyrus took a trip to sign contracts with the builders. He met with manufacturers in Ohio, Michigan, Wisconsin, and Illinois. Soon these states would be the main grain producers in the country.

The most important contract was with A. C. Brown. He planned to build two hundred reapers in Cincinnati, Ohio.

By fall 1844, Cyrus returned to Walnut Grove with sales of four hundred to five hundred reapers. He would bring in a profit of at least eight thousand dollars. During this time, Cyrus never admitted that his father was the original inventor of the reaper. Cyrus continued to patent improvements under his own name. On January 31, 1845, he received a patent for McCown's two-way serrated blade and a blade support invented by Leander.

Meanwhile, Mr. McCormick and Leander worked on building a raker seat for the reaper. Until this time, a worker would walk quickly beside the machine as the reel piled grain onto the platform. The worker had to rake the heavy wheat from the machine's platform to the ground. The job might be easier if the worker could sit on the machine. But the reel was in a place where a seat might go.

Mr. McCormick thought he had found a good position for the seat. Cyrus was thrilled. He was in Cincinnati at the time. He wanted workers at A. C. Brown to start adding raker seats to the reapers right away. But Cyrus soon received word that the raker seat failed in field tests back in Walnut Grove. The position of the seat wasn't right. So Cyrus started experimenting with a raker seat in Brown's shops.

Meanwhile, Leander solved the problem and sent Cyrus details and drawings of a different way to attach the seat. Cyrus claimed that Leander's ideas were similar to his own. In fact, Cyrus said that his own design worked better. He patented the raker seat improvement in his own name. This added feature increased sales. But Cyrus never gave Leander credit.

5

Success in Chicago

Leander wasn't happy that Cyrus took credit for the raker seat. But what could he do? His father had given the reaper to Cyrus, and Cyrus had kept his promise. All the McCormicks were making money from the invention. So Leander kept quiet.

Cyrus traveled during much of 1845 to check up on production sites. At the A. C. Brown factory in Cincinnati, work was running far behind. Cyrus really wanted Leander at the factory to supervise. Leander wasn't sure he liked this idea. On October 22, 1845, Leander married Henrietta Hamilton, the daughter of a wealthy landowner. Leander's financial situation greatly improved after his marriage. He didn't need to work for Cyrus. Plus, Leander knew that Cyrus would take credit for any more improvements to the reaper. No, Leander wouldn't go to Cincinnati. He would stay and work with his father in Walnut Grove.

In 1846 Cyrus again employed John McCown to make blades for the McCormicks. Cyrus wrote his brother William, asking him to keep McCown happy. In two years, Cyrus would have to renew his patent on the reaper. He would need to prove that his reaper was invented and used in 1831. And he couldn't renew his patent if McCown claimed the two-way serrated blade as his own invention. Cyrus worried about McCown.

Meanwhile, Mr. McCormick had become ill in 1846. One winter night, fire blazed in one of his shops. He rushed from the house without putting on warm clothes. After months of ill health, Robert McCormick died on July 4. His wife and all his children, except Cyrus, surrounded his deathbed. Cyrus was still traveling in the West at the time. He was heartbroken when he heard the news.

After his father's death, Cyrus continued to urge Leander to go to Cincinnati. Cyrus decided to offer his brother a greater share of the profits. Leander decided it was a good deal. He became a one-third partner in the business. Leander started working at Brown's factory. He hired and fired workers. He also checked for bad materials and corrected poor construction. Leander got along well with everyone. He was friendly and efficient.

While Leander went to Cincinnati, Cyrus joined William at Walnut Grove to help build a few reapers. William was happy to have his brother home. William didn't have the mechanical talents of Leander or his father. And apparently Cyrus didn't have the skill either. The thirty-five machines built at Walnut Grove had to be scrapped. None of them worked properly when tested. The failed reapers were the last to come out of the Walnut Grove factory. Cyrus decided to build the machines closer to the grain-producing states of the West.

Cyrus thought the new factory should be located in Chicago, Illinois. The United States had recently gained new territory after a war with Mexico. Immigrants and easterners were rushing west to grab the land. At that time, Chicago had only 17,000 people and a few paved streets. But the city was near Lake Michigan. Cyrus thought the lake breezes made the city a healthy place to live. Chicago had telegraphs for better communication and railways for transportation. Cyrus's company would stand near rivers and canals, making it easy to ship his machines to other states.

In 1847 Cyrus joined Charles M. Gray to form a reaper business under the company name of McCormick & Gray. Gray had already been building

McCormick reapers and paying Cyrus license fees. The new partners began construction of their Chicago factory. The McCormick reaper was in demand. Cyrus planned to produce five hundred reapers in the new factory for the 1848 harvest.

On January 19, 1848, Cyrus applied to the U.S. Patent Office to extend his reaper patent. Back at Walnut Grove, he and his brother William tracked down witnesses for a hearing on the patent. The witnesses agreed to swear that the McCormick reaper existed in 1831. The date was important. It meant that Cyrus's machine had been in use before Hussey patented his machine. Cyrus needed to prove that his reaper came first.

No one at the patent office doubted that Cyrus had invented the reaper. But if they thought he didn't invent it, Cyrus would not get the patent extension. So he had been careful when gathering statements from witnesses. Cyrus didn't ask witnesses to say that he *invented* the reaper. Instead, he asked them to state that he had *constructed* the machine.

At a hearing on March 17, Cyrus questioned his witnesses for the record. But they were not all believable. Cyrus lost his fight for the patent extension. Other businesspeople could now manufacture the reaper model patented in 1834.

But Cyrus still had the only rights to the two-way serrated knife and raker seat inventions. No one else could build the reaper with these features. And these improvements made the McCormick reaper stand out from its competition.

Workers had nearly completed the new factory by the time Cyrus returned to Chicago. Soon the plant was humming. The factory met its goal, cranking out five hundred machines in time for the 1848 harvest. But Cyrus had some differences over money with his new partner. Gray decided to sell his part of the company. Soon Cyrus owned the entire business.

Cyrus hoped that Leander would leave Cincinnati and run the Chicago factory. He offered Leander a one-sixth share in the business. Leander took him up on the offer and moved to Chicago. William came from Walnut Grove to work as an assistant. Cyrus was happy to have his brothers by his side.

Production at the Chicago McCormick factory grew fast. Workers built 1,500 reapers for the 1849 harvest and 1,600 for the 1850 harvest. Cyrus bought new machinery and hired more workers. In 1851 Cyrus ended all his licensing deals. The McCormick reapers all came out of the Chicago plant. The city's newspapers called the McCormick factory the largest of its kind in the world.

The McCormicks also found another way to improve the reaper. It could mow grass as well as cut grain. Most farmers grew both, but they couldn't afford to buy two machines. The McCormicks solved this problem by adding a mowing attachment to the reaper.

With production moving along well, Cyrus turned his full attention to sales. He developed a team of salesmen who would travel to farms across the region. The salesmen supervised the delivery of the machines. Many were mechanics who could set up the machines and make sure they worked properly. The salesmen kept spare parts on hand to repair machines. This service was a big help. During the harvest, farmers didn't have time to waste on repairs.

The sales team sent Cyrus reports about the best selling methods. He learned that farmers often didn't read the reaper advertisements in the newspapers and magazines. Posters called broadsides worked better. The salesmen tacked the broadsides onto fences. Sometimes local country stores used the broadsides to wrap up goods for customers.

During the harvest season, Cyrus and his brothers traveled throughout the wheat country. They enjoyed getting away from the factory for a while. And these trips gave them a chance to watch the machines at work. They always looked for ways to improve the reaper. They talked to the farmers, who thought it was an honor to have a McCormick visit.

By this time, Cyrus had a deluxe reaper machine built. An American eagle decorated its frame. He took out an English patent on this reaper and sent the machine to the Great Exhibition of 1851 in London. This world's fair featured all kinds of new inventions. At first the English weren't too impressed with Cyrus's reaper. The *London Times* called the reaper a combination of a flying machine, wheelbarrow, and chariot. But at the fair, Cyrus's reaper won the Council Medal, the highest award for an invention.

Farmers in other countries started taking an interest in mechanical harvesting. Inventors in the United States sent their reapers to the International Exposition in Paris. The McCormick reaper was there, along with those of Hussey, John S. Wright, and John H. Manny. Cyrus won the Grand Gold Medal in Paris. News of his outstanding machine spread quickly. Soon people all over Europe knew of Cyrus McCormick.

Back in the United States, Cyrus had to fight legal battles against his competitors. Their reapers included some of the features patented for the McCormick reaper. But they hadn't paid for these rights. Many competitors thought Cyrus didn't deserve an extension on his patents. They thought he had too much of the reaper market for himself. They said it wasn't fair for Cyrus to control the reaper business like that. By 1856 Cyrus had placed almost 16,000 reapers, reaper-mowers, and mowers on farms in the United States.

6

Love, War, and Fire

Cyrus traveled on business more than ever while Leander and William ran the factory. When Cyrus was in Chicago, he attended services at North Presbyterian Church. There he noticed a new voice in the choir. It belonged to Miss Nancy Fowler. Cyrus was taken with her immediately. He spent more and more time in Chicago to be with Nettie, as he called her. Cyrus and Nancy married in a small ceremony on January 26, 1858. Cyrus was forty-eight years old, and Nancy was twenty-two.

The newlyweds traveled to Washington, D.C., for their honeymoon. Cyrus continued to fight his patent battles there. In the end, he lost. Cyrus was upset and disappointed. But he tried not to let it bother him too much. After all, he had built a name for himself and for his reaper. He had done his best and thanked God for all his good fortune.

On May 16, 1859, Nancy gave birth to Cyrus Jr. The family celebrated this joyous event. But trouble was brewing among the McCormick brothers. Leander and William saw how much money Cyrus was making and thought it was unfair. William was unhappy because the long hours of indoor work at the factory were making him ill. Leander wanted credit for the reaper improvements and threatened to resign.

Cyrus knew his brothers worked hard, and he needed them. In November 1859, Cyrus signed a twelve-year agreement with his brothers. Leander and William would each receive $5,000 a year and a share of the profits. The company became known as Cyrus H. McCormick and Brothers. But Leander and William weren't true partners in the company. As part of the agreement, Cyrus would have the right to patent all improvements that Leander made.

By this time, Cyrus was a millionaire—one of the few millionaires in the United States. He was famous around the country and in many other parts of the world. Cyrus enjoyed his wealth, but he also enjoyed using his money to help others. He gave large sums of money to those in need and took a special interest in helping the Presbyterian Church.

Cyrus was sure his good fortune would continue. Farming was booming in the prairie states. New fertilizers and improved seeds increased the size of harvests. Demand for the reaper grew. But in the spring of 1861, the orders for reapers slowed. The Northern states were fighting the Southern states in the Civil War (1861–1865). Farmers seemed more interested in the battles raging in the East than in harvesting their grain. Even the McCormick salesmen were quitting their jobs to join the fight. Soon there were fewer men to harvest the grain. Cyrus used this fact in his advertising campaign. As farms lost workers, reapers became more important.

Tensions continued to grow between Cyrus and his brothers. Leander and William believed that Cyrus was taking advantage of them. On November 1, 1864, Cyrus agreed to join in a real partnership with his brothers. William and Leander would each own one-fourth of McCormick and Brothers. But William's health changed everything. He suffered from nervous headaches and depression. On his deathbed, he begged Cyrus and Leander to work together in harmony. William died on September 27, 1865.

Over the next few years, it grew harder and harder for Leander to work with Cyrus. Leander's wealth had grown because of the business. Like Cyrus, he had bought real estate all over Chicago. But Leander was still upset about Cyrus taking all the credit for the reaper's success. These feelings gnawed at Leander as he went about his work at the factory.

As the business grew, the danger of fire at the factory also increased. Over the years, many small fires started. Wood, paint, and oil filled the building. Sparks from the factory chimneys or from the steamboats on the river could start a blaze. So the McCormicks installed fireproof doors and had workers sweep up wood shavings as quickly as possible. All new buildings were brick. Cyrus also shipped machines as soon as possible. In case of fire, fewer reapers would be destroyed. He hired watchmen to make rounds day and night to check for fires.

In 1866 the McCormicks bought insurance on the raw materials and stock of machines at the plant. The insurance company would pay the McCormicks if fire or another disaster destroyed this property. In 1870 the McCormicks insured the factory buildings for a small amount. But nothing could prepare the McCormicks for the Great Chicago Fire of October 1871. Fire swept through the city, destroying everything in its path. Flames turned the McCormick factory to ruins. The brothers' homes and their other real estate burned to the ground. Most of Chicago lay smoldering.

Cyrus was in the city at the time, but his wife and Cyrus Jr. were away on vacation. They returned to

Chicago two days after the fire to find Cyrus weary and wearing a partially burned coat. The family stood in line at the Third Presbyterian Church to get bread and blankets. They slept on mattresses on the floor of a hotel crowded with people.

The fire didn't crush Cyrus's spirits. He immediately started to rebuild the factory and set up a temporary office. An iron vault that held the business's records survived the fire. Cyrus found the list of farmers who owed the McCormicks money. When crops had failed, the company had given farmers extra time to pay their bills. This time, Cyrus needed help from the farmers. He sent out a notice asking them to pay their debts right away.

Meanwhile, workers cleared away debris and tried to save machine parts. They scrambled to construct a temporary factory before winter. The fire destroyed almost two thousand harvesting machines. Luckily, the salesmen had four thousand machines outside the city to sell for the 1872 harvest season. By 1872 the temporary factory was ready to produce three thousand reaper-mowers for the next harvest. That same year, Leander's son, Robert Hall, became a partner in the company. He owned one-sixteenth of the business.

Soon a new McCormick factory rose in Chicago. The best equipment filled the plant's four large buildings. Steam heated the factory, and gas powered the lights. The McCormicks moved ahead with production of the reapers. Soon they added binders to the machines. This new part would automatically bind the wheat with wire or twine. Farmers no longer had to tie the bundles by hand. Cyrus bought or licensed binder patents and other improvements to keep the McCormick machines up to date.

In 1874 tragedy struck the prairie states. Millions of grasshoppers invaded. They ate through crops on farms from Texas to Minnesota. Many farmers lost their entire crop. That meant hard times for farm families. Cyrus didn't hesitate to help the farmers who'd lost everything. He sent money to them through the salesmen. He gave all the farmers extra time to pay their bills.

In Chicago trouble continued between Cyrus and Leander. In 1879 Cyrus Jr. graduated from Princeton College. He was ready to enter the business. But Leander didn't think it was right for Cyrus Jr. to have a higher position than his own son, Robert Hall. Leander threatened to leave the company. He and his son planned to start their own harvesting machine factory. But Cyrus and Leander finally came to an agreement. Their firm would be known as the McCormick Harvesting Machine Company. Cyrus would own three-quarters of the company. Leander and Robert Hall, together, would own one quarter.

On January 1, 1880, the *Chicago Tribune* ran an article about Cyrus. It praised his success in Europe, where he had received several awards. But Cyrus's success angered someone in Chicago. The Chicago magazine *Factory and Farm* printed an article that asked "Was McCormick the Inventor of the Reaper?" Cyrus couldn't believe it! Someone was publicly questioning his claim as inventor of the reaper. Who was responsible for this article? Could it have been Leander and Robert Hall? No one knows for sure.

But on February 18, 1880, Cyrus complained to the board of directors of his company, a group that supervised the overall business. He accused Leander and Robert Hall of being disloyal to the business. On April 14, the board voted. They wanted Leander and Robert Hall out of the company. Robert Hall resigned, but Leander would not leave.

Leander's refusal could have led to a big legal battle in the courts. But somehow the brothers settled the matter privately. For the next four years, there was no public arguing in the McCormick family. Leander continued as vice president of the company.

By this time, Cyrus had moved his family into a house on Rush Street. Besides Cyrus Jr., he and

Nancy had four more children—Mary, Anita, Harold, and Stanley. Cyrus still spent most of his time working. But his health wasn't always good. Sometimes illness kept him from doing things. As Cyrus grew older, he didn't exercise much and was bothered by severe colds, a sore throat, and pain in his joints.

Finally, old age caught up with Cyrus. He was seventy-five years old when he gathered his family around his bedside one May morning in 1884. He held the hands of each of his children. Together, they prayed and sang hymns. Cyrus no longer thought about his reaper business or his great wealth. Someone asked Cyrus if he wanted anything. He answered that he only wanted heaven. His last thoughts were of God. Cyrus Hall McCormick died on May 13, 1884, leaving behind a loving family and a great legacy.

More about Cyrus Hall McCormick

The reaper stands as one of the most important inventions of the 1800s. Cyrus Hall McCormick's life work of making and selling reapers thrust farmers into the modern age of machines. Cyrus was also a pioneering businessperson. With his force of salesmen, he offered farmers free trials, money-back guarantees, and easy payment plans. And he educated farmers on the use of his product. Other business leaders learned from Cyrus's successes and used his methods.

After Cyrus died, Cyrus Jr. took charge of the business. In 1902 the company joined with several other farm equipment companies to form the International Harvester Company. Cyrus Jr. became its first president. Soon the company also made tractors, which replaced horses in the fields.

Cyrus's success benefited the entire McCormick family, just as his father had wanted. But Leander and his children still wanted Robert McCormick to be known as the inventor of the reaper. A sixty-one-page booklet, *Memorial of Robert McCormick*, appeared a year after Cyrus died. It is believed that Leander's son, Robert Hall McCormick, wrote it.

No matter how people remember Cyrus McCormick, the fact remains that he realized his dreams. He built a successful business. He provided farmers with the best reaper he could. His machine freed workers from the fields. And through his work, Cyrus gave farmers the means to succeed and helped them live out their own dreams.

The McCormick Reaper of 1831

The harvesting machine that Cyrus McCormick tested in 1831 was pulled by a horse. This reaper had seven important elements:

Rotating reel: This part pulled the grain stalks into the machine.

Knife: The grain stalks fell against a straight knife, which moved back and forth.

Fingers or guards for the knife: These held the grain stalks during the cutting action.

Platform: The cut grain fell onto the platform.

Main wheel: This wheel turned directly behind the horse. It supplied power for the reel and knife.

Forward side draft: The horse walked in front of the wheel and to the side of the machine, so the knife could cut the standing grain.

Divider bar: This bar was at the outer end of the knife. It helped separate grain to be cut from the rest of the standing grain.

Two workers operated the machine. One rode the horse. The other raked the cut grain from the platform to the ground. Other workers gathered the cut grain into bundles and tied them with twists of grain.

Selected Bibliography

Casson, Herbert N. *Cyrus Hall McCormick: His Life and Work*. Chicago: A. C. McClurg & Co., 1909.

"Grain Harvesting History." *Shenandoah Valley Agricultural Research & Extension Center.* http://www.vaes.vt.edu/steeles/mccormick/harvest.html (Sept. 1, 2005).

Hafstad, Margaret R., ed. *Guide to the McCormick Collection of the State Historical Society of Wisconsin*. Madison: State Historical Society of Wisconsin, 1973.

Hutchinson, William T. *Cyrus Hall McCormick: Harvest, 1856–1884*. New York: Appleton-Century Company, 1935.

Hutchinson, William T. *Cyrus Hall McCormick: Seed-Time, 1809–1856*. New York: The Century Co., 1930.

Lyons, Norbert. *The McCormick Reaper Legend: The True Story of a Great Invention*. New York: Exposition Press, 1955.

McCormick, Cyrus. *The Century of the Reaper*. Boston: Houghton Mifflin Company, 1931.

"The McCormick Reaper Patent." *New York Times*, July 6, 1861, 4.

Steward, John F. *The Reaper: A History of the Efforts of Those Who Justly May Be Said to Have Made Bread Cheap*. New York: Greenberg Publisher, 1931.

Index

McCormick, Mary Caroline (sister), 8
McCormick, Robert (father): as a businessman, 16–17, 26–27; death, 40; and iron-work, 9; and inventing, 7–8, 15; and the reaper, 16–17, 27–28, 30, 34–37
McCormick, Stanley (son), 57
McCormick, William (brother), 8, 41, 44–45, 50–51
McCormick, William S. (cousin), 15, 17
McCown, John, 31, 40
Mechanics' Magazine, 23–24
Memorial of Robert McCormick, 58

North Presbyterian Church, Chicago, 49–50

patents, 16–17, 23–24, 31, 36–37, 42–43, 46–47, 49, 55

R. & C. H. McCormick, 27
reaper: changes, 19, 23–24, 31, 35–37, 45, 55; competition, 23–24, 29, 32–34; development of, 13, 15–17, 28–29; Hussey and, 23–24, 33–34, 46; ideas about, 12, 31; patent rights for, 35–36; sales, 34–37, 44–46, 50–51
Richmond, Virginia, 23, 32

Robert McCormick & Son, 16–17, 26
Rockbridge County, Virginia, 8

Semi-Weekly Whig, 35
slaves, 10, 19, 30
Southern Planter, 32
South River Farm, 26–27
Staunton, Virginia, 12

Turner, the Reverend Jesse W., 32
two-way serrated knife, 31, 36, 44

United States Patent Office, 17

Walnut Grove, 8, 10, 15, 26, 28, 34–35, 41
Washington, D.C., 16–17, 49
Wright, John S., 46

About the Author

Catherine A. Welch is an award-winning author who has written numerous books, including biographies, histories, and science books. A former science teacher, she was inspired to begin writing for children after reading to her own two sons. She is an instructor with the Institute of Children's Literature and lives in Southbury, Connecticut.

About the Illustrator

Jan Naimo Jones has been a professional illustrator for over 25 years. She studied illustration at Kendall School of Design, and she has worked on many books for young people. She has also been an elementary-school art teacher and a mural painter at homes and churches. She lives in Grand Rapids, Michigan, where her art and her seven kids keep her very busy.